Transformations in Nature

A Caterpillar Becomes a Butterfly

Amy Hayes

Cavendish
Square

New York

Published in 2016 by Cavendish Square Publishing, LLC
243 5th Avenue, Suite 136, New York, NY 10016

Website: cavendishsq.com

This publication represents the opinions and views of the author based on his or her personal experience, knowledge, and research. The information in this book serves as a general guide only. The author and publisher have used their best efforts in preparing this book and disclaim liability rising directly or indirectly from the use and application of this book.

CPSIA Compliance Information: Batch #CW16CSQ

All websites were available and accurate when this book was sent to press.

Cataloging-in-Publication Data

Hayes, Amy.
A caterpillar becomes a butterfly / by Amy Hayes.
p. cm. — (Transformations in nature)
Includes index.
ISBN 978-1-5026-0824-6 (hardcover) — ISBN 978-1-5026-0822-2 (paperback) — ISBN 978-1-5026-0825-3 (e-book)
1. Butterflies — Juvenile literature. 2. Butterflies — Metamorphosis — Juvenile literature. 3. Caterpillars — Juvenile literature. I. Hayes, Amy. II. Title.
QL544.2 H39 2016
571.8'15789—d23

Editorial Director: David McNamara
Copy Editor: Rebecca Rohan
Art Director: Jeffrey Talbot
Designer: Stephanie Flecha
Senior Production Manager: Jennifer Ryder-Talbot
Production Editor: Renni Johnson
Photo Research: J8 Media

The photographs in this book are used by permission and through the courtesy of: Giles DeCruyenaere/Shutterstock.com, ChameleonsEye/Shutterstock.com, cover; StevenRussellSmithPhotos/Shutterstock.com, 5; Ed Reschke/Photolibrary/Getty Images, 7; Eileen Tanson/Science Source/Getty Images, 9; Don Farrall/Digital Vision/Getty Images, 11; Ron Brancato/E+/Getty Images, 13; Scott Tysick/Oxford Scientific/Getty Images, 15; Stephen J. Krasemann/All Canada Photos/Getty Images, 17; Melola/Shutterstock.com, 19; Jeff Lepore/Photographer's Choice RF/Getty Images, 21.

Printed in the United States of America

Contents

Where do **butterflies** come from?

4

A butterfly starts as an egg on a leaf.

7

The egg hatches
into a **caterpillar**!

A caterpillar is born
very hungry.

11

It eats leaves to help it grow.

13

Then, the caterpillar turns itself into a **pupa**.

15

The pupa builds itself a sack called a **cocoon**.

17

After a few days, the cocoon breaks open.

19

The caterpillar has turned
into a beautiful butterfly!

21

New Words

butterflies (BUT-tur-flyz) Insects that fly in the daytime with brightly colored wings.

caterpillar (KAT-ur-pill-er) A larva, the second stage of butterflies and moths.

cocoon (ka-KOON) A sack of silk that larvae form around themselves during the pupa stage.

pupa (PEW-pa) Insects in a transformation stage, usually inside a cocoon.

Index

About the Author

Amy Hayes lives in the beautiful city of Buffalo, New York. She has written several books for children, including *Hornets, Medusa and Pegasus, From Wax to Crayons*, and *We Need Worms!*

About BOOKWORMS

Bookworms help independent readers gain reading confidence through high-frequency words, simple sentences, and strong picture/text support. Each book explores a concept that helps children relate what they read to the world they live in.